"Oak, Rock, Moon" Oil • 8" h x 16" w

Yes!
MAKE
Art
MATTER

An Artist's View of Santa Cruz

Scenic Spots to Visit and Enjoy

Lidia C. Hasenauer

First Printing
ISBN-13: 978-1468172065
ISBN-10: 1468172069

Cover and "Oak, Rock, Moon" photos by Guy Siratt

This book is dedicated to my husband Kevin,
daughter Julia and son Ethan.
They make Santa Cruz a truly beautiful place to live.

Contents •

Contents

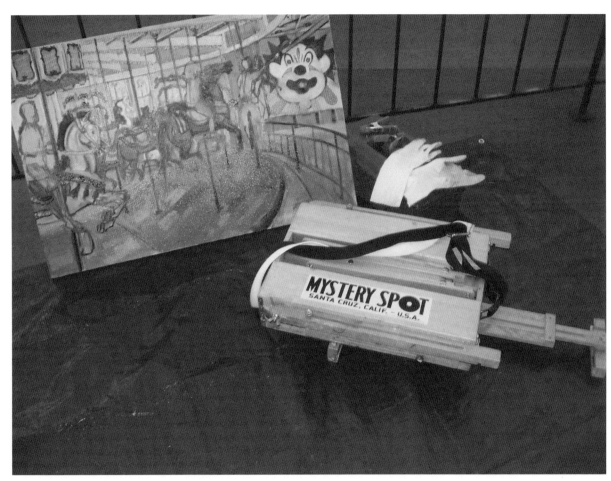

My trusty French easel, paint box and work in progress.

Introduction ·

This is a book of paintings featuring places in and around Santa Cruz, California. If you are interested in seeing these views for yourself, I have included notes and maps on where to find them. Next to the maps are points of interest near the painting site.

Most of the locations are close to town. The places I have painted on-site are a short hike from the road. This is necessary for me when I carry my painting equipment. The set up includes: A folding French easel (that I wear like a back pack), a canvas, and a paint box.

Santa Cruz has many beaches and parks to enjoy. It is located on the Monterey Bay which is a marine sanctuary. The coastal beauty of Santa Cruz is surrounded by mountains and redwood forests. No matter what the weather is like, there is always a place to go. I've captured some of the spots I like in this collection of paintings. The following pages will take you to the Santa Cruz I've been lucky enough to know and portray.

Lidia C. Hasenauer

• •

The Santa Cruz Harbor Area

● **Location:** Seabright Beach

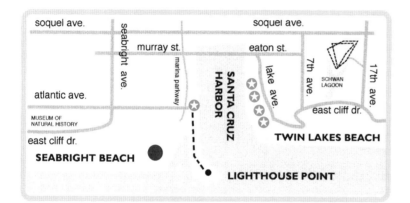

✪ **Visit and Enjoy:**
Restaurants at the harbor.

Note: You can walk on a path to the lighthouse. The entrance to the harbor is on one side of the jetty and the beach on the other. There are several restaurants located at the harbor to grab a bite to eat after a stroll on the beach.

Photo: Guy Siratt

Painting: "The Black Dog" • Oil • 24"h×30"w

The Santa Cruz Harbor Area

● **Location: Lighthouse Point at Seabright Beach**

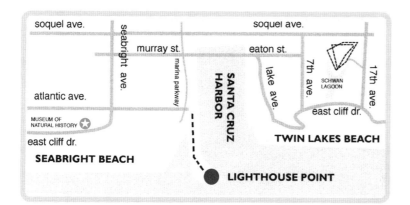

✪ **Visit and Enjoy:**
The Santa Cruz Museum
of Natural History.

....

Note: This fellow and his unicycling group were showing off
their unique balancing skills. He is on the huge cement "jacks"
that encircle the jetty at the Walton Lighthouse in Seabright.
Don't try this stunt to impress your friends.

Painting: "Unicycle" • Oil • 36"hx40"w

Photo: Lidia C. Hasenauer

The Santa Cruz Harbor Area

● **Location:** Santa Cruz Harbor

✪ **Visit and Enjoy:**
A cruise from the harbor.

Note: The path that leads to the Walton Lighthouse has a great view of boats leaving and entering the harbor. The harbor is an active place for those who love to sail, kayak, row or stand-up paddle. There is also a path around the harbor that offers a view of the docks for the "landlubbers".

Photo: Paul Titangos

Painting: "Red Life Jackets" • Oil • 16"h×18"w

The Santa Cruz Harbor Area

● Location: Twin Lakes Beach

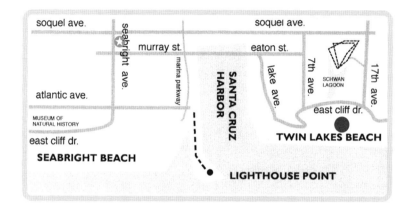

✪ Visit and Enjoy:
The Santa Cruz Roller Palladium.

Note: This is a good place for a day in the sun and a picnic. The water is fairly calm, which makes it a great location to take the family for a day out at the beach.

Photo: Guy Siratt

Painting: "Lifeguard Station #4" • Oil • 10"h×10"w

The Santa Cruz Harbor Area

● Location: Schwan Lagoon

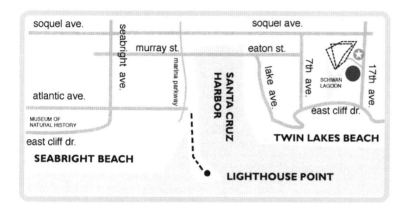

○ Visit and Enjoy:
The Simpkins Swim Center.

Note: This is a nice walk or short bike ride to take with the family. The trail leads you past some old oak trees and a view of Schwan Lagoon. The trail starts behind the Simpkins Swim Center off of 17th Avenue.

Photo: Lidia C. Hasenauer

Painting: "Fog on Schwan Lagoon" • Oil • 18"hx24"w

The Boardwalk and More

● **Location:** Santa Cruz Beach Boardwalk

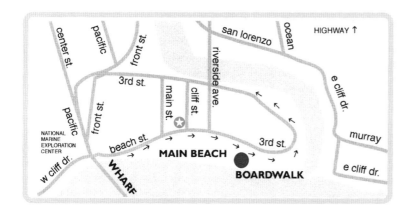

✪ Visit and Enjoy:
The Boardwalk Bowl.

Note: Throw a ring into the clown's mouth while riding a hand carved wooden carousel horse. The clown will light up and ding if you make it! The ring toss is a rare and fun feature of the Looff Carousel. This painting was created on location in honor of the carousel's 100th anniversary.

Painting: "Reaching for the Ring" • Oil • 24"h x 36"w

The Boardwalk and More

● Location: Santa Cruz Beach Boardwalk

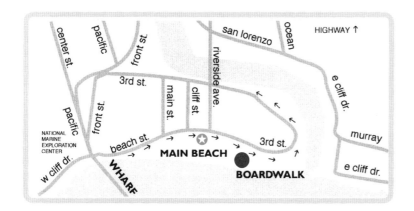

✪ Visit and Enjoy:
Neptune's Kingdom
and play miniature golf,
arcade games, pool, and
air hockey.

Note: The antique carousel horses are well taken care of by the conservator, Jimmy. I was able to capture him at work. This painting was created using four colors: magenta, french ultramarine blue, cadmium yellow and white.

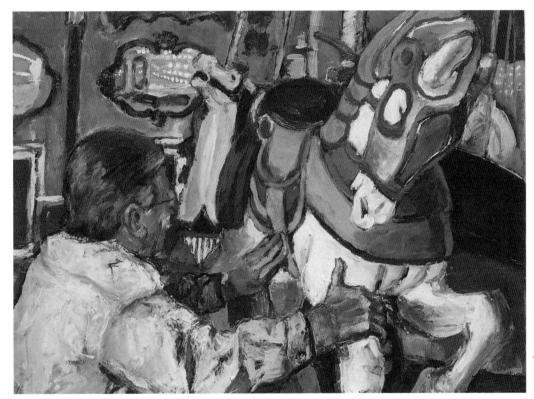

Photo: Guy Siratt

Painting: "The Conservator at the Looff Carousel" • Oil • 24"h×30"w

The Boardwalk and More

● **Location: East Cliff Drive**

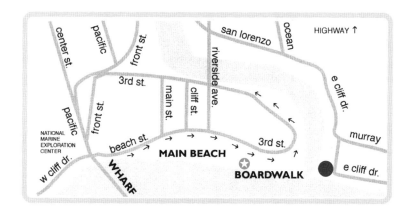

❂ **Visit and Enjoy:**
The Giant Dipper Wooden
Roller Coaster built in 1924.

Note: This view is at a small park located on a cliff overlooking
Main Beach. The painting was created on site in honor of the
100th anniversary of the Santa Cruz Beach Boardwalk. A storm
has since downed the trees in the foreground of the painting
leaving an unobstructed view of the Giant Dipper Roller Coaster.

Photo: Paul Titangos

Painting: "Twists and Turns by the Sea" • Oil • 24"hx36"w

The Boardwalk and More

● Location: Main Beach

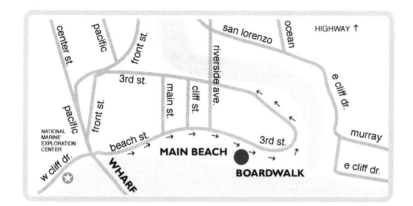

✪ Visit and Enjoy:
Surfboard rentals and surf lessons at Cowell's Beach.

Note: After having fun at the Boardwalk, enjoy yourself at Main Beach. During the summer there are concerts on the beach every Friday at sunset.

Photo: Lidia C. Hasenauer

Painting: "Boardwalk Morning Fog" • Oil •18"hx24"w

The Boardwalk and More

● **Location: The Santa Cruz Wharf**

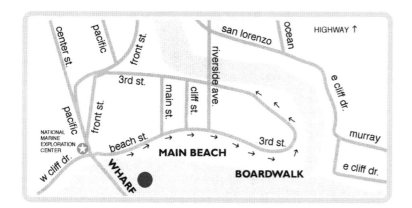

✪ **Visit and Enjoy:**
The National Marine
Exploration Center.

Note: There are many restaurants and shops to visit on the wharf. Treat yourself to an ice cream cone and pick up some souvenirs. There are two viewing areas cut out of the end of the wharf to look down on the sea lions resting on its supports.

Photo: Paul Titangos

Painting: "The Evening Shift" • Oil • 36"h×36"h

The Boardwalk and More

● **Location: Beach Hill**

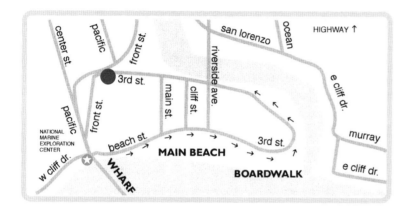

○ Visit and Enjoy:
Running the annual Wharf to Wharf race which starts at the Santa Cruz Wharf and ends at the Capitola Wharf.

Note: Every year in spring the Santa Cruz Classic Criterium takes place at Beach Hill. This is a pretty exciting, sharp turn for the riders. The Amgen Tour of California also rode this route in 2010.

Photo: Guy Siratt

Painting: "Front and Third Street" • Oil • 18"h×36"w

The Downtown Area

● **Location:** Downtown at Cooper Street and Pacific Avenue

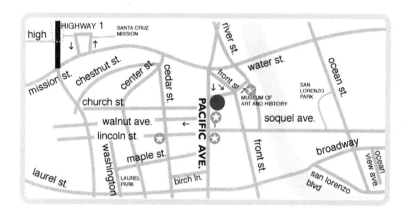

✪ **Visit and Enjoy:**
The movie theatres downtown.

Note: Take a walk on Pacific Avenue and explore downtown Santa Cruz. After visiting the shops and grabbing a bite to eat, treat yourself to an evening movie or some live music. The stairs on the left lead to the Museum of Art and History.

Painting: "Cooper Street" • Oil • 16"hx18"w

The Downtown Area

● **Location:** Downtown behind Front Street

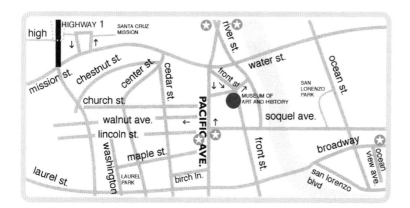

✪ **Visit and Enjoy:**
Art galleries in and around downtown.

Note: The Museum of Art and History is a pretty lively place. On the first Friday of the month downtown Santa Cruz celebrates the arts. The museum, galleries and stores host receptions to promote art hanging on their walls. When the purple jacaranda trees bloom in June, they add to the existing local color.

Photo: Guy Siratt

Painting: "Jacaranda Tree at the Museum of Art and History" • Oil • 24"hx18"w

The Downtown Area

● **Location: Laurel Park**

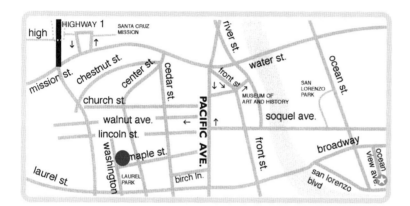

✪ **Visit and Enjoy:**
The double slide at
Oceanview Park.

Note: Laurel Park is located near downtown Santa Cruz
on Maple Avenue. The maple trees drop extra large orange
leaves in fall. There is a playground for children in the park.

Photo: Lidia C. Hasenauer

Painting: "Laurel Park" • Oil • 36"hx24"w

The Downtown Area

● **Location: Kuumbwa Jazz Center**

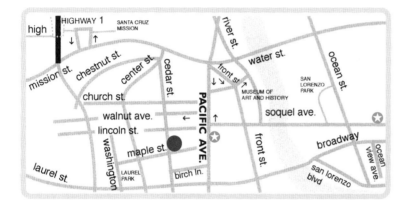

✪ **Visit and Enjoy:**
Music clubs in the Santa Cruz area.
For listings check out:
    Good Times Santa Cruz
    Santa Cruz Metro
    Santa Cruz Sentinel

Note: Musicians from around the world come to play in Santa Cruz. There are several venues in town that offer a variety of musical styles. The crowds are smaller than other Bay Area locations and the sound is excellent. This painting was made from a drawing I did while watching a show.

Painting: "Trio at the Kuumbwa" • Oil • 36"hx36"w

The Downtown Area

● **Location: Holy Cross Church and Mission Santa Cruz**

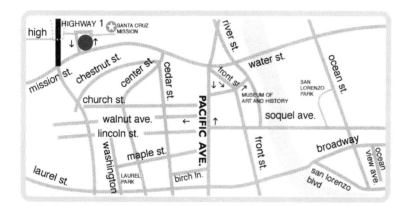

✪ Visit and Enjoy:
The garden at Mission Santa Cruz.

Note: Holy Cross Catholic Church is one of the promi-
nent landmarks you will see driving down highway 17
from the north. It was built in 1889 over what used to be
Mission Santa Cruz. Next door to the church are some of
the original mission buildings. Mission Santa Cruz was the
12th of 21 missions created in California by the Spanish
between 1769 and 1823.

Photo: Paul Titangos

Painting: "Holy Cross Church" • Oil Study on Paper • 5"hx7"w

The Downtown Area

● **Location: The bridge over Highway 1, High Street entrance**

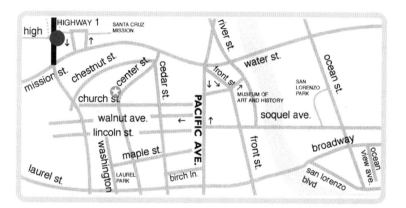

✪ Visit and Enjoy:
Events at the Santa Cruz
Civic Auditorium.

Note: This is a bike-friendly bridge. It has a short but
steep circular climb instead of stairs. It is one of the many
ways to travel from the downtown area to the west side
of Santa Cruz. The bridge crosses Highway 1 right before
Mission Street.

Painting: "The Bridge Over Highway 1" • Oil • 36"hx24"w

The West Side

● **Location:** Neary Lagoon, at the California and Bay Avenue entrance

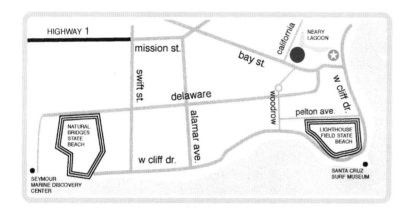

✪ **Visit and Enjoy:**
The animals and plants that live at the lagoon.

. . . .

Note: Neary Lagoon is a wildlife sanctuary located behind a water purification plant. To get to it, pass through a children's playground, walk behind the tennis courts, enter a gate and go down the hill. Tour the lagoon via the water "walkway" that starts on the left.

Photo: Lidia C. Hasenauer

Painting: "Neary Lagoon" • Oil Study on Paper • 10"h×16"w

The West Side

● Location: West Cliff Drive

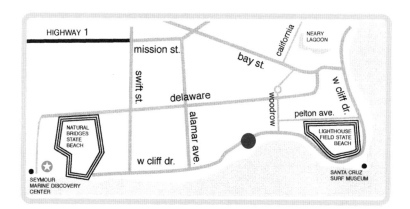

✪ Visit and Enjoy:
The Aquarium at the Seymour
Marine Discovery Center.

Note: West Cliff Drive provides a pleasant walk or bike
ride along the coast. This is a lengthy stretch of coastline
that starts at the Santa Cruz Beach Boardwalk and ends at
Natural Bridges State Park. There is parking all along this
route so you can start where you like. Juggling is optional.

Photo: Lidia C. Hasenauer

Painting: "The Juggler on West Cliff Drive" • Oil • 24"h×30"w

The West Side

● **Location:** Dog Beach/ Its Beach, West Cliff Drive

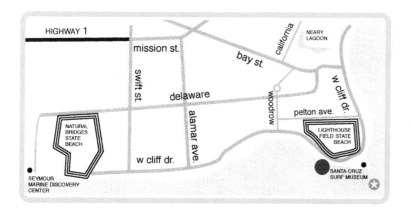

✪ **Visit and Enjoy:**
The sea lions resting on Seal Rock.

Note: This beach is a good destination for four-footed friends. The lighthouse on the cliff behind the dogs houses the Santa Cruz Surf Museum. The point overlooks Steamer Lane, where international surfing competitions are held.

Painting: "Everybody Plays with Sticks" • Oil • 6"hx6"w

Photo: Guy Siratt

The West Side

● **Location: Light House Field, West Cliff Drive**

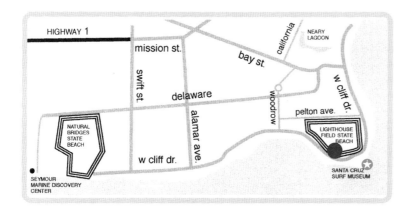

❖ **Visit and Enjoy:**
The surfers catching waves at Steamer Lane.

Note: Lighthouse Field is a home to migrating Monarch butterflies in the winter. If you walk close to the trees you can see them packed up against each other. The Santa Cruz Surf Museum houses a collection of surf memorabilia from the past 100 years of surfing.

Photo: Lidia C. Hasenauer

Painting: "The Surf Museum from Lighthouse Field" • Oil Study on Paper • 16"hx11"w

The West Side

● Location: Mitchell's Cove, West Cliff Drive

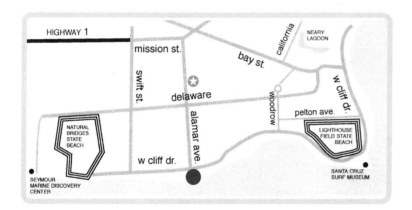

✪ Visit and Enjoy:
Garfield Park on Alamar Avenue.

Note: If you are walking on West Cliff Drive, Mitchell's
Cove is another place to stop and view the ocean. The
beach is fairly small and washes out during high tide.
When I painted this I had to pay attention behind me or
the waves would have taken my easel as the tide rose!

Photo: Paul Titangos

Painting: "Mitchell's Cove" • Oil • 24"h×30"w

The West Side

● Location: Natural Bridges State Park, West Cliff Drive

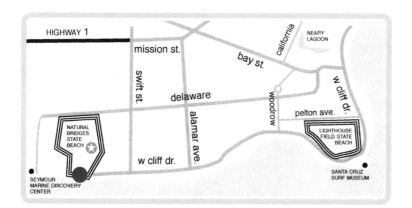

● Visit and Enjoy:
The Monarch butterfly grove.

....

Note: This is a nice beach to spend a little time relaxing.
The orange sunset light against the rocks is remarkable.
Natural Bridges is named after the hole in the rock that
causes a "natural bridge" over the water. There used to be
two bridges, but the one on the left has eroded over time.
Explore the park's Visitor Center and the Monarch butterfly grove nearby.

Photo: Lidia C. Hasenauer

Painting: "Natural Bridges" • Oil Study on Paper • 11"h×16"w

The West Side

● **Location: Pogonip Park**

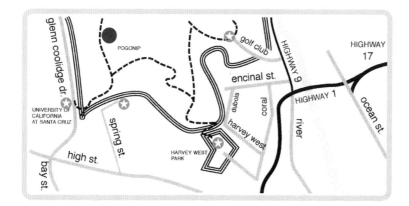

○ **Visit and Enjoy:**
Pogonip Park from various trail heads:
    Golf Club Dr.
    Harvey West Park
    Spring St. (limited parking residential)
    UC Santa Cruz upper campus

Note: This trail is part of the many trails of Pogonip Park.
Dogs are welcome on leash. There are many chances to
observe wildlife in the park.

Photo: Lidia C. Hasenauer

Painting: "Pogonip Trail" • Oil Study on Paper • 11"hx16"w

Wilder Ranch State Park

● **Location:** Victorian Farm House, Wilder Ranch State Park

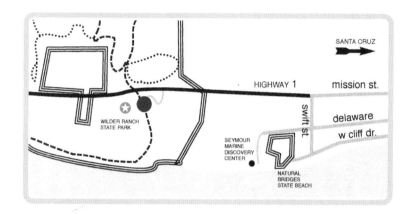

✪ **Visit and Enjoy:**
A tour of the Victorian home on weekends.

Note: Wilder Ranch is a preserved dairy farm from the 1800's. The park offers living history demonstrations where volunteers answer questions about the house, the water-powered machine shop and the blacksmith's forge.

Photo: Paul Titangos

Painting: "Wilder Ranch House" • Oil •16"hx18"w

Wilder Ranch State Park

● **Location: Main Barn, Wilder Ranch State Park**

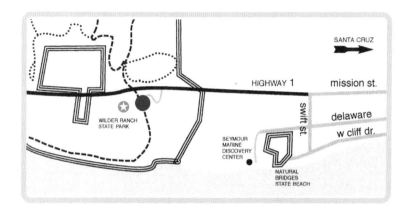

❂ **Visit and Enjoy:**
Draft horse wagon rides during living demonstration days.

Note: The Victorian barn at Wilder Ranch has some wonderful architectural details inside and out. During park hours the barn is left open for visitors to view. Goats and sheep are kept behind the gate on the right of the barn. The building to the right is the Visitor Center.

Painting: "Old Barn and Eucalyptus Tree" • Oil • 18"hx24"w

Wilder Ranch State Park

● **Location: Entrance, Wilder Ranch State Park**

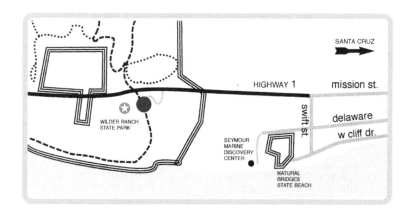

✪ **Visit and Enjoy:**
A picnic on the Wilder Ranch grounds.

Note: Wilder is surrounded by coastal farmland. Several different crops are farmed around this park. Hawks and other birds of prey can be spotted hunting for mice in the fields.

Photo: Lidia C. Hasenauer

Painting: "Rows of Rosemary" • Oil on Paper • 12"hx18"w

Wilder Ranch State Park

● **Location: Cliff Path, Wilder Ranch State Park**

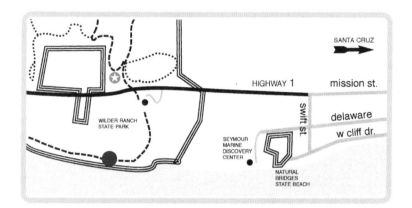

✪ Visit and Enjoy:
A hike in the hills above the ranch.

Note: The cliff path is great for walking, jogging or riding a bike. The views of the ocean and surrounding cliffs are dramatic. There are a couple of small beaches to explore along the path.

Photo: Paul Titangos

Painting: "View from Coast Trail" • Oil on Board • 12"hx16"w

Wilder Ranch State Park

● **Location:** Private Stable Off of Wilder Ranch Equestrian Trail

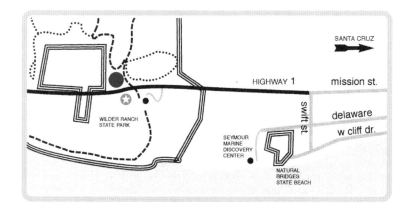

○ **Visit and Enjoy:**
The ranch gardens.

Note: Bring your horse to Wilder Ranch! Wilder offers equestrian riding trails, as do other parks in the county. You can ride past the old barn on the previous page and take a trail that leads to the hills across the highway. The young lady in the painting is riding an Icelandic horse.

Photo: Guy Siratt

Painting: "Bareback Riding at Sunset" • Oil • 24"h×30"w

AN ARTIST'S VIEW OF SANTA CRUZ

The University of California at Santa Cruz

● **Location:** Quarry Road off of Hagar Road, UCSC Farm Garden:
The Center for Agroecology and Sustainable Food Systems

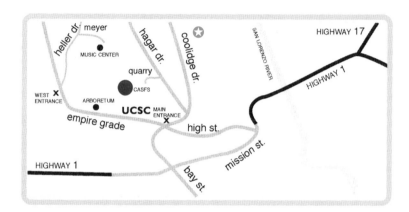

✪ **Visit and Enjoy:**
The view of Santa Cruz and
the Pacific Ocean.

Note: This is a peaceful walk for those who like to garden.
If you are looking for this particular view, the persimmons
ripen in November and December. The garden is open
seven days a week.

Painting: "Persimmons at UCSC Farm Garden" • Oil • 24"h×18"w

The University of California at Santa Cruz

● Location: Quarry Road off of Hagar Road, UCSC Farm Garden:
The Center for Agroecology and Sustainable Food Systems

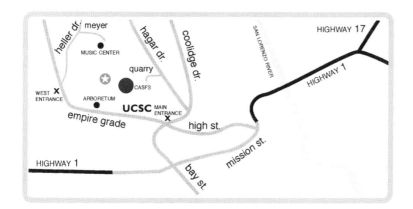

✪ Visit and Enjoy:
The CASFS Life Lab that features
a chicken coop, a human sundial,
an observation bee hive, and
a musical tree.

Note: Another feature of the UCSC farm garden is the
native birds. There are many birds of prey that hunt in this
area. While I was painting this, two birds of prey perched
on the tree, a golden eagle and a kestrel.

Photo: Guy Siratt

Painting: "Cacti and Kestrel" • Oil on Panel • 24"h x 12.5"w

The University of California at Santa Cruz

● **Location:** Quarry Road off of Hagar Road, UCSC Farm Garden:
The Center for Agroecology and Sustainable Food Systems

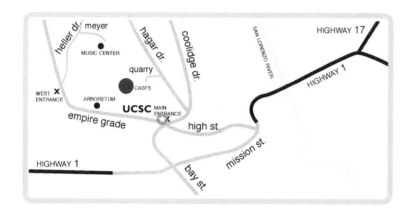

❂ **Visit and Enjoy:**
The Farm and Garden Market Cart
in early June through October to
buy fresh vegetables and fruits at
the corner of Bay and High Street.

Note: The Center for Agroecology and Sustainable Food
Systems is 25 acres of farming beauty along the coast. It is a
research and education facility aimed at advancing farming
techniques. Organic methods are used to enhance growth
production while preserving the existing environment.

Photo: Lidia C. Hasenauer

Painting: "Row of Onions" • Oil on Paper • 6"h×9"w

The University of California at Santa Cruz

● **Location: Behind the Music Center**

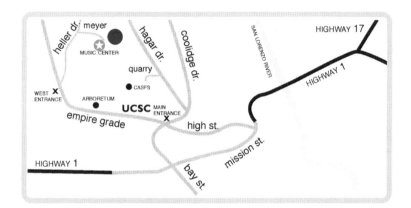

✪ **Visit and Enjoy:**
Concerts at the UCSC Music Center.

Note: To get to this spot take the West Entrance to UCSC located on High Street. Once you turn onto Heller Drive, continue until you reach Meyer Drive and make a right into the parking area. The trail is behind the Music Center.

Photo: Guy Siratt

Painting: "Oak Trail" • Oil • 8"hx16"w

The University of California at Santa Cruz

● **Location: Behind the Music Center**

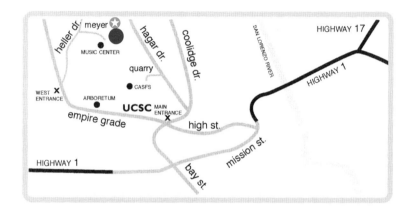

○ **Visit and Enjoy:**
Shakespeare Santa Cruz productions that are performed at the UCSC MainstageTheater and outdoors at the Sinsheimer-Stanley Festival Glen.

Note: UC Santa Cruz has some beautiful coastal views overlooking the Monterey Bay. The campus is built around meadows and redwood trees. You may see some deer while driving through the college.

Photo: Paul Titangos

Painting: "Trail and the Sea" • Oil • 12"hx18"w

The University of California at Santa Cruz

● **Location:** University of Santa Cruz Arboretum

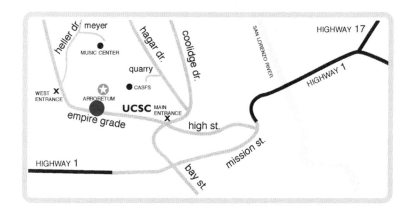

✪ **Visit and Enjoy:**
Norrie's Gift Shop at the Arboretum.

Note: The Arboretum has paths that wind through its many gardens. Walking through the large collection of specimens from California, Australia, New Zealand, South Africa and Chile is a treat for the eyes.

Photo: Lidia C. Hasenauer

Painting: "Cactus Garden at the Arboretum" • Oil Study on Paper • 11"h×16"w

Capitola and Aptos

● **Location: Capitola Village**

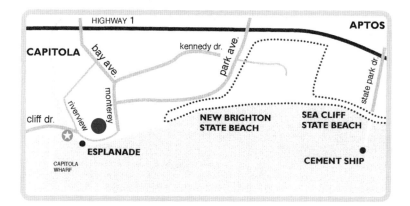

◎ Visit and Enjoy:
The annual Begonia Festival where floats decorated with colorful begonia flowers sail under the bridge on Labor Day Weekend.

Note: The Stockton Bridge crosses the San Lorenzo River as it empties into the Pacific Ocean. There is a small path along the river for a peaceful walk. Enjoy the beach, shops and restaurants that Capitola has to offer.

Painting: "Stockton Bridge, Capitola" • Oil Study on Paper • 11"hx16"w

Capitola and Aptos

● **Location: Capitola Village**

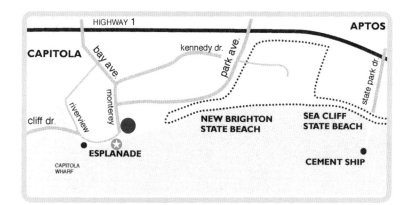

○ **Visit and Enjoy:**
Summer twilight concerts at the beach on Wednesday nights.

Note: These steps are located at the back of a parking lot at the Esplanade at Capitola Beach. There are great views of Capitola from the top. Take a walk on the cliff path after catching your breath.

Painting: "Elevation, Capitola Steps" • Oil • 24"h×36"w

Photo: Lidia C. Hasenauer

AN ARTIST'S VIEW OF SANTA CRUZ

Capitola and Aptos

● Location: Sea Cliff State Beach, Aptos

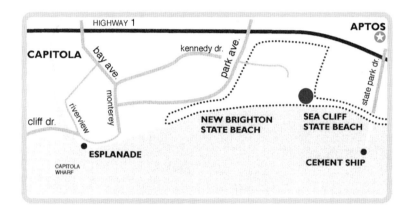

❂ Visit and Enjoy:
Hike, bike or horseback ride at
The Forest of Nisene Marks State Park
and visit the epicenter of the 1989
Loma Prieta Earthquake.

Note: If you would like to take a long stroll on a beach, try both New Brighton Beach and Seacliff State Beach. Seacliff State Beach is located beyond the pier in this painting. The pier is unusual because of the cement ship scuttled at the end of it. This used to be an amusement center in 1929, with carnival booths, a dance hall, a restaurant and swimming pool.

Photo: Lidia C. Hasenauer

Painting: "Sand Pipers and the Cement Ship" • Oil • 8"h×10"w

Scenic Spots Near Town

● **Location:** Henry Cowell Redwoods State Park
north of Santa Cruz

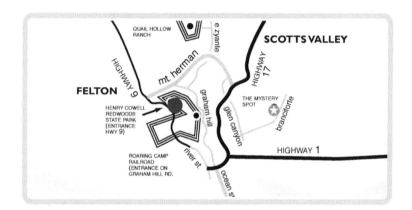

✪ **Visit and Enjoy:**
The gravity defying Mystery Spot.

Note: Henry Cowell State Park should be on your list of places to visit in Santa Cruz. Once in the park you can walk the easy loop trail and see the largest redwood trees around. One man-made feature of the park is the steam train at Roaring Camp Railroad. Take a train ride through the redwoods or to the Boardwalk.

Photo: Lidia C. Hasenauer

Painting: "Westside Junction" • Oil • 16"hx18"w

Scenic Spots Near Town

● Location: Quail Hollow Ranch County Park
north of Santa Cruz

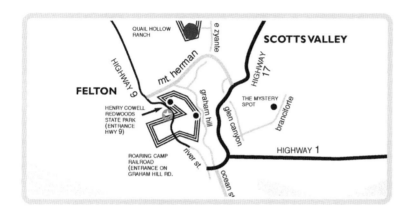

✪ Visit and Enjoy:
The Bigfoot Discovery Museum.

Note: Quail Hollow Ranch is an excellent place for a picnic.
It also has hiking trails and equestrian trails. There is a Visitor
Center that has displays about the natural surroundings and
cultural history of the park.

Painting: "Geese at Quail Hollow" • Oil • 10"h×8"w

Scenic Spots Near Town

● Location: Davenport on the beach side of Highway 1
             north of Santa Cruz

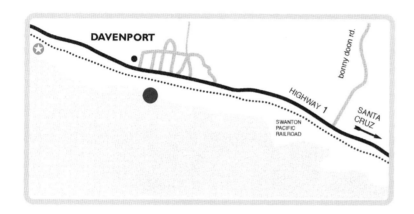

✪ Visit and Enjoy:
Wind surfers and kite surfers at
Waddell Beach then hike across the
way at Rancho Del Oso Park
located 17 miles from Santa Cruz.

Note: This is a view of the Swanton Pacific Railroad with the
old CEMEX cement plant in the background. Once you
cross the railroad tracks you can find a path to walk along
the cliffs. There are several good restaurants in Davenport
across the highway from this site.

Photo: Guy Siratt

Painting: "Rocks and Rail" • Oil • 8"hx16"w

Scenic Spots Near Town

● **Location:** Moss Landing Harbor off of Highway 1
south of Santa Cruz

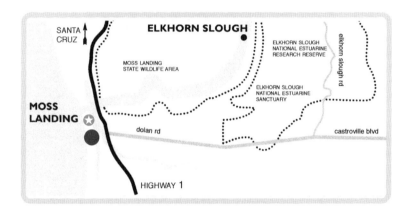

✪ Visit and Enjoy:
Moss Landing's restaurants and
antique shops.

Note: A great tour of Elkhorn Slough goes out of this harbor.
You can also explore the slough by renting a kayak. More
than 200 species of birds use the slough to rest during their
annual migrations. Sea lions, harbor seals and otters make
Elkhorn Slough their home.

Photo: Guy Siratt

Painting: "Otters Moss Landing" • Oil • 28"h×32"w

Scenic Spots Near Town

● Location: Elkhorn Slough, Moss Landing
            south of Santa Cruz

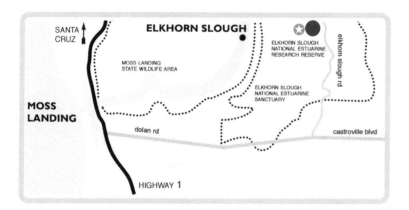

❂ Visit and Enjoy:
The Visitor Center and docent led walking tours of the slough.

Note: There are 5 miles of hiking trails that lead to fascinating views of the inhabitants of the slough. Such places as Hummingbird Island, and the Rookery, where blue herons, great egrets and double-crested cormorants nest, make for a rewarding hike and great photo opportunities. The painting was created at the park entrance, where these hikes begin.

Photo: Guy Siratt

Painting: "Elkhorn Slough" • Oil Study on Paper • 5.5"h×18"w

Scenic Spots Near Town

● Location: Pigeon Point, north of Santa Cruz

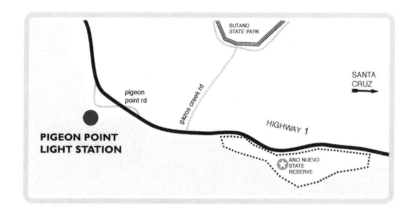

BUTANO
STATE PARK

SANTA
CRUZ
→

pigeon
point rd

gazos creek rd

HIGHWAY 1

PIGEON POINT
LIGHT STATION

AÑO NUEVO
STATE
RESERVE

✪ Visit and Enjoy:
Elephant seals at Año Nuevo
State Reserve during winter.

Note: Pigeon Point Lighthouse is a hostel and working light-house. It is one of the tallest in America. At the beach below are tidepools. Spend an afternoon searching for the sea creatures that live at the shore. The cyclists in the painting were heading back to Santa Cruz to complete the Big Kahuna Triathlon, which is an annual event.

Photo: Guy Siratt

Painting: "Cyclists Passing Pigeon Point" • Oil • 24"hx36"w

Acknowledgements ....

Many thanks to:

My husband Kevin and children Julia and Ethan for your love and support; my painting and drawing buddies for keeping me inspired: Sally Ne-Smith, Angelina Medina (pictured in straw hat), Stacey Pollard, Kimberly Parrish, Judy Johnson, Carolyn Blackman (pictured in pink hat) Andrew Purchin, and Kit Eastman; Christy Blessing, Mary Blessing and Kim Albridge for their encouragement; photographers Paul Titangos and Guy Siratt; my art teachers at El Camino College: William Brownlee, Robert Kobashi, Andy Fagan, Willie Suzuki, David Patterson and Harrison Storms; and Noah Buchanan who's art classes I took at the University of California at Santa Cruz and Cabrillo College in Santa Cruz.

Thanks to Mary Anne Carson from Santa Cruz County Bank, curator Joan Blackmer, and publicist for the Santa Cruz Beach Boardwalk Brigid Fuller for making it possible to paint the Looff Carousel on-site; curators Karen Kienzle and Susan Hillhouse Leask for including me in the 2007 Plein Air Affaire at the Museum of Art and History where I created the painting of the Giant Dipper Roller Coaster.

I would like to acknowledge the writings of Julia Cameron and Eric Maisel. Their books on creativity are the voices of experience and understanding. They have helped me often.

To those who have chosen to hang my art in their homes and offices I am honored that my paintings share your lives. Thank you.

Photo: Lidia C. Hasenauer

Painting: "Angie and Carolyn painting at Natural Bridges"
Oil on Paper • 8"h×11"w

Final Note •••••••••••••••••••••••••••••••••

Dear Reader,

Thank you for reading this book. The people I have included in my paintings are real, and they did the things that I rendered. The community of Santa Cruz can be as inspiring as the landscape! It has been a pleasure visually recording it all. I hope you get the opportunity to visit the places I've painted.

- Lidia

Photo: Guy Siratt

Photo: Lidia C. Hasenauer

Painting above: "New Leaf Market" • Oil • 24"wx18"h

Painting left: "Civilization/Rio Theater" • Oil (detail) • 24"wx36"h

Drawing left top: "The Great Morgani" • Charcoal (detail) • 18"wx24"h

• •

About the Artist

Lidia has been painting in oils and exhibiting her work since 1993. She lives with her family in Santa Cruz, California.

Check out her website and more paintings at: LidiaStudio.com

19043569R00058

Made in the USA
Charleston, SC
04 May 2013